This Password Book
Belongs To

REMEMBER: Keep This Book Safe!

Website	Username	Password

Website	Username	Password

Website	Username	Password

Website	Username	Password

Website	Username	Password

Website	Username	Password

Website	Username	Password

Website	Username	Password

Website	Username	Password

Website	Username	Password

Website	Username	Password

Website	Username	Password

Website	Username	Password

Website	Username	Password

Website	Username	Password

Website	Username	Password

Website	Username	Password

Website	Username	Password

Website	Username	Password

Website	Username	Password

Website	Username	Password

Website	Username	Password

Website	Username	Password

Website	Username	Password

Website	Username	Password

Website	Username	Password

Website	Username	Password

Website	Username	Password

Website	Username	Password

Website	Username	Password

Website	Username	Password

Website	Username	Password

Website	Username	Password

Website	Username	Password

Website	Username	Password

Website	Username	Password

Website	Username	Password

Website	Username	Password

Website	Username	Password

Website	Username	Password

Website	Username	Password

Website	Username	Password

Website	Username	Password

Website	Username	Password

Website	Username	Password

Website	Username	Password

Website	Username	Password

Website	Username	Password

Website	Username	Password

Website	Username	Password

Website	Username	Password

Website	Username	Password

Website	Username	Password

Website	Username	Password

Website	Username	Password

Website	Username	Password

Website	Username	Password

Website	Username	Password

Website	Username	Password

Website	Username	Password

Website	Username	Password

Website	Username	Password

Website	Username	Password

Website	Username	Password

Website	Username	Password

Website	Username	Password

Website	Username	Password

Website	Username	Password

Website	Username	Password

Website	Username	Password

Website	Username	Password

Website	Username	Password

Website	Username	Password

Website	Username	Password

Website	Username	Password

Website	Username	Password

Website	Username	Password

Website	Username	Password

Website	Username	Password

Website	Username	Password

Website	Username	Password

Website	Username	Password

Website	Username	Password

Website	Username	Password

Website	Username	Password

Website	Username	Password

Website	Username	Password

Website	Username	Password

Website	Username	Password

Website	Username	Password

Website	Username	Password

Website	Username	Password

Website	Username	Password

Website	Username	Password

Website	Username	Password

Website	Username	Password

Thank you!

I hope you've
enjoyed my notebook.
Please leave a review.

www.ingramcontent.com/pod-product-compliance
Lightning Source LLC
Chambersburg PA
CBHW070848070326
40690CB00009B/1745